ALPACA FARMING SUCCESS

A Step-By-Step Guide To Raising And Breeding Alpacas

Turn Your Passion for Alpacas into a Profitable Venture with Expert Husbandry Techniques

Dr. Fabian Felicity

CHAPTER ONE

Introduction

Alpacas are native to South America and have grown in popularity across the globe due to their gentle attitude, fine fleece, and potential as livestock.

Whether you're a seasoned farmer or a novice in the world of animal husbandry, knowing alpacas is crucial before going on the adventure of raising these distinctive animals. In this inquiry, we'll look at the fundamentals of alpaca care, from choosing the proper breed to providing a pleasant and safe habitat for them.

Understanding Alpacas

Alpacas, a member of the camelid family, are related to llamas, guanacos, and vicuñas. Alpacas, known for their beautiful, soft fleece, are mainly bred for their fiber, which comes in a range of natural hues.

Their wool, known as alpaca fiber, is hypoallergenic, lightweight, and has exceptional thermal characteristics, making it very desirable in the textile industry.

In addition to their treasured fleece, alpacas are known for their kind personalities. They are gregarious creatures that flourish in the company of their kind. Keeping them in pairs or small groups promotes their well-being and reduces loneliness-related stress. Furthermore, alpacas are kind and easy to teach, making them ideal for people of all ages.

Alpacas are herbivores that eat grass and hay. Adequate nutrition is critical for their well-being, as is access to fresh water and adequate forage. Understanding their food requirements is critical to sustaining their general health and productivity.

Choosing The Right Alpaca Breed.

Choosing the right alpaca breed for your farm is an important choice that will determine the success of your endeavor. There are two primary breeds: Huacaya and Suri. The Huacaya alpaca, known for its rich and crimped fleece, is the more common of the two. The Suri alpaca, on the other hand, has long, silky hair that hangs down from its body in distinctive, twisted bundles.

Each breed has its own set of benefits, and the decision is typically based on personal tastes and particular aims. Suri alpacas, for example, might be an excellent option for creating beautiful, silky wool with a distinct drape.

If you're looking for a traditional, fluffy fleece that's easy to process, the Huacaya breed may be a better fit.

Consider the alpaca's hue, since its fleece comes in a variety of tints, including white, brown, black, and gray.

Color not only enhances the visual appeal of your alpaca farm, but it may also affect the market value of their fiber. Understanding market demand for various hues is critical for making sound breeding selections.

Setting Up Your Alpaca Farm

Building a successful alpaca farm involves meticulous planning and attention to detail. Begin by ensuring that your alpacas have enough area to graze, exercise, and socialize. Fencing is essential for creating safe enclosures and protecting your alpacas from predators. Additionally, sufficient drainage is required to avoid waterlogging in the fields.

Temperature, humidity, and ventilation all have an impact on the health of alpacas, which flourish in a temperate environment. Adequate shelter is required to keep them safe from adverse weather conditions. When designing your alpaca farm, consider the local environment and build shelters that give plenty of shade in the summer and protection from hard winter winds.

Routine veterinarian treatment is vital for keeping your alpacas healthy. Establish a connection with a qualified veterinarian who can provide immunizations, do routine check-ups, and advise on diet and parasite treatment. Prompt medical intervention may help avoid illness spread and keep the herd healthy.

CHAPTER TWO

Building Suitable Alpaca Shelters

Alpaca shelters, often known as barns or sheds, are vital for protecting your alpacas from the weather. Building adequate shelters requires careful consideration of the local temperature, the quantity of alpacas in your herd, and their requirements.

Alpaca shelters should be designed to provide sufficient ventilation while also protecting from rain, snow, and intense sunshine. Alpacas want enough room to move freely and lay peacefully. Additionally, the flooring should be non-slippery to avoid injuries, and frequent cleaning is required to maintain a sanitary atmosphere.

In colder areas, adequate insulation and heating are critical to avoiding temperature-related stress. In contrast, in warmer areas, ventilation is critical to allowing alpacas to naturally cool down. Monitoring and changing the temperature inside the shelter is critical to improving the health of your alpacas.

To summarize, alpaca farming requires a holistic strategy that includes understanding the nature of these unique animals, choosing the proper breed, and establishing a favorable environment for their well-being. The voyage starts with a full knowledge of alpacas, who are valued not just for their fleece but also for their gentle and friendly temperament.

Choosing the correct alpaca breed is a critical choice that will impact the success of your enterprise. Whether you choose the Huacaya or Suri breed, each has unique characteristics that may be used depending on your tastes and aims.

Furthermore, paying attention to color and market demand will help your alpaca farm become more commercially viable.

Setting up an alpaca farm requires thorough preparation, from procuring enough acreage and fencing to building appropriate shelters that cater to the special requirements of these animals. Adequate veterinary care, regular check-ups, and a focus on nutrition are all important aspects of good alpaca management.

Ultimately, effective alpaca farming requires a combination of expertise, compassion, and attention to detail. Understanding alpacas, selecting the proper breed, and providing an environment that promotes their well-being set you on a path that not only provides financial rewards but also enables you to build a gratifying relationship with these fascinating animals.

Nutritional Requirements Of Alpacas

Alpacas, known for their lustrous fleece and sensitive nature, need a well-balanced and nutritious food to stay healthy. Understanding alpacas' dietary demands is critical for their general health and production. These South American camelids have evolved to severe surroundings, therefore their diet should mirror their natural grazing patterns.

Forage And Pasture

Forage, including grasses and legumes, is the cornerstone of an alpaca's diet. Alpacas are natural grazers, so ensuring access to high-quality pasture is critical. Pasture rotation is advised to avoid overgrazing and provide a steady supply of new food. Owners should monitor pasture quality to avoid exposure to poisonous weeds, which may harm alpaca health.

Hay And Supplementary Foods

In addition to pasture, alpacas may need additional hay, particularly during seasons of low fodder quality or shortage. Alpacas are often fed high-fiber grass hay.

Monitoring their physical condition and modifying the quantity of hay provided is critical for preventing obesity or malnutrition. Commercial alpaca diets may also be offered, as long as they match the animals' unique nutritional needs.

Minerals And Vitamin Supplements

Alpacas need enough mineral and vitamin supplements to stay in good condition. Calcium, phosphorus, copper, zinc, and selenium are among the most common deficits. Owners should contact a veterinarian to develop a well-balanced supplement diet that takes into account local soil conditions and the makeup of available forage.

CHAPTER THREE

Water Consumption

Alpacas need enough fluids to maintain good health. Always give clean and accessible water. Alpacas may lower their water intake during the winter months, therefore it is important to check their water consumption and take precautions to avoid dehydration.

Healthcare And Veterinary Considerations

Alpacas need proactive treatment and frequent veterinarian attention to be healthy. Owners should be aware of prevalent health conditions and take preventative actions to preserve a healthy herd.

Parasite Control

Internal parasites, such as worms, maybe a serious hazard to alpaca health. Regular fecal testing and deworming regimens are critical elements of parasite management. Pasture management, which includes rotational grazing and waste collection, may assist in reducing parasite exposure.

Vaccinations

Vaccinations are critical for preventing communicable infections that might afflict alpacas. Clostridial illnesses, respiratory infections, and some viral disorders are among the most important immunizations. Creating a vaccination program in conjunction with a veterinarian is critical for protecting the herd from any outbreaks.

Routine Health Checks

Regular health inspections enable owners to detect possible problems early. Routine health evaluations include monitoring physical condition, evaluating behavior, and looking for indicators of lameness or dental issues. Owners should build a connection with a trained veterinarian who can advise on preventative care and respond quickly to any health issues.

CHAPTER FOUR
Alpaca Breeding: Principles And Practices

Breeding alpacas requires a full grasp of reproductive concepts and appropriate breeding techniques. Successful breeding requires careful planning, genetic considerations, and suitable care for both male and female alpacas.

Reproductive Physiology

Alpacas are induced ovulators, which means that females produce eggs in reaction to mating. Understanding the reproductive physiology of alpacas is essential for effective breeding. Owners should be conversant with the female alpaca's estrous cycle and receptivity signals, which will help them to time breeding efforts correctly.

Genetic Considerations

Selective breeding is used to improve desired qualities and preserve genetic variation in alpaca herds. Breeders should understand the genetic features they want to encourage, whether it's fleece quality, color, or conformation. Responsible breeding methods include avoiding mating with close relatives to limit the danger of genetic problems.

Pregnancy Care

Once successfully mated, pregnant alpacas need extra attention to ensure a safe pregnancy. Adequate feeding, regular veterinarian care, and a stress-free environment are essential during this time. Owners should be ready for any issues and have a birthing plan in place.

Caring For Pregnant Alpacas

Pregnancy in alpacas is a sensitive phase that requires close monitoring to preserve the health of both the dam and the growing cria. Caring for pregnant alpacas requires proper feeding, monitoring, and birth preparation.

Nutrition While Pregnant

Pregnant alpacas have higher food needs to support their developing cria. It is critical to modify one's diet to include more energy, protein, and important nutrients. Regular veterinarian check-ups may assist ensure that the pregnant alpaca receives appropriate nourishment and remains healthy during the gestation period.

CHAPTER FIVE

Monitoring Pregnancy

Regular monitoring of pregnant alpacas is required to identify any possible problems early on. Ultrasound exams may confirm pregnancy and reveal possible difficulties. Monitoring weight increase, bodily condition, and behavioral changes enables owners to respond quickly if any issues occur.

Birthing Preparedness

Preparing for the birth process, known as "cria delivery," is critical. Owners should prepare a clean and peaceful setting for the upcoming delivery, offer a pleasant birthing place, and be available to help if necessary. Familiarity with typical birthing patterns and signals of discomfort is critical for a healthy birth.

To summarize, recognizing and meeting the dietary, healthcare, and reproductive requirements of alpacas is crucial for sustaining a healthy and happy herd. By concentrating on these critical areas, alpaca owners may secure their animals' well-being and help the survival of this unique and valued species.

The Alpaca Birthing Process

The alpaca birthing process is an important part of alpaca husbandry and requires considerable attention and preparation. Alpacas, famed for their gentle disposition and rich fleece, usually give birth to a single cria, however, twins are not uncommon. Alpacas have an 11-month gestation period, and as the birthing season approaches, pregnant females must be closely monitored.

Preparing For Birth

During the weeks before delivery, alpaca owners must provide a pleasant and safe environment for their pregnant alpaca, often known as a dam. Adequate shelter, clean bedding, and access to fresh water are all necessary. Additionally, owners should be aware of indicators of approaching labor, including as restlessness, frequent getting up and laying down, and the emergence of a mucous plug.

The Birthing Process

When labor starts, alpacas normally give birth during the day, and the procedure takes around 30 to 60 minutes. Alpaca owners should keep a safe distance and only intervene if issues emerge. Following birth, the dam normally cleans the cria, and it is critical that the newborn alpaca wakes up and begins feeding within a few hours to get vital colostrum.

Post-Birth Care

Post-birth care entails carefully monitoring both the mother and the child. Adequate nutrition for the dam is essential for milk production, and frequent veterinarian check-ups protect the health of both mother and baby. Alpaca crias must be socialized with people and other alpacas to develop a feeling of security within the herd.

CHAPTER SIX

Raising Alpaca Crias (Youngsters)

Raising alpaca crias requires a mix of devoted care, correct feeding, and socializing to maintain their health and growth. The first weeks are critical for forming a deep link between the cria and its human caretakers.

Nutrition

Proper nutrition is essential for raising alpaca crias. They first depend on their dam's nutrient-dense milk, but as they develop, the addition of high-quality hay and pellets becomes necessary. Adequate vitamin and mineral supplements may be required to ensure healthy development.

Socialization

Socializing alpaca crias is critical to their mental and emotional development. Spending time with them, touching them gently, and introducing them to other alpacas in the herd all help them become well-adjusted and friendly. This approach helps to reduce stress-related behaviors and maintains a calm and cooperative temperament.

Weaning

Weaning alpaca crias usually happens at about six months of age, however, this might vary. Throughout this phase, it is critical to check the crias for indications of stress and provide extra assistance as required. Separating them from their mothers gradually and exposing them to a diet free of maternal milk helps to ensure a seamless transition.

Fiber Harvesting And Processing

Alpacas are admired for both their mild demeanor and their lustrous wool. To produce high-quality end products, alpaca fiber must be harvested and processed with care and by best practices.

Harvesting

The major source of alpaca fiber is their yearly shearing, which usually occurs in the spring. Shearing not only gives a new start to the growth season but also guarantees that the alpacas have a compassionate and comfortable experience. Skilled shearers use strategies that emphasize the animal's well-being while extracting the most useful fiber.

Sorting & Cleaning

After shearing, the obtained fleece is meticulously sorted to separate the fibers by quality and color. Cleaning follows, which includes the removal of dirt, oil, and vegetable debris. Thorough cleaning is required to produce a high-quality final result, which is normally accomplished by gentle washing and rinsing.

CHAPTER SEVEN

Spinning And Weaving

After cleaning and sorting, the fiber is ready to be processed into yarn or cloth. Spinning converts raw alpaca fiber into yarn of varying thicknesses and textures. Weaving yarn into fabric or creating completed objects needs expertise and attention to precision.

Alpaca Shearing Techniques

Alpaca shearing is a specialist technique that protects the animals' well-being while increasing the output of high-quality wool. Proper technique and a sympathetic attitude make for a stress-free experience for both the alpacas and the shearers.

Tools & Equipment

Alpacas must be sheared using particular instruments, such as electric clippers developed for fiber animals and different combs and brushes. Well-maintained equipment ensures that the shearing process runs smoothly and efficiently. The shearing area should be clean, well-lit, and well-ventilated.

Handling Techniques

Alpaca shearing requires a calm and delicate technique. Experienced shearers know how to handle alpacas so that they are neither stressed nor uncomfortable. Proper restraining procedures, such as secure chutes or tables, help to provide a safe and regulated environment for both the animals and the shearers.

After-Shearing Care

Alpacas need extra attention after shearing to adjust to their new short form. Alpacas may be more sensitive to temperature fluctuations, therefore adequate shelter and protection from the weather are needed. Monitoring their health and administering any required post-shearing therapies ensures a smooth recovery.

Using Alpaca Fiber: Products And Markets

Alpaca fiber's flexibility and exquisite features make it a popular material for a wide range of items.

Understanding the market and developing new ways to use alpaca fiber is critical for alpaca farmers looking to optimize the value of their production.

Fiber Products

Alpaca fiber is used to make a variety of things, including clothes, accessories, and household goods. Alpaca fiber, which is soft, lightweight, and hypoallergenic, is renowned for its warmth and durability. Scarves, sweaters, and blankets produced from alpaca fiber are popular among customers looking for high-quality, sustainable, and ethically sourced items.

Niche markets.

Alpaca growers might take a strategic strategy by exploring specialized markets. Hand-spun yarn, handcrafted fabrics, and unique fiber mixes are examples of specialty commodities that cater to specific customer tastes. To get access to these specialized markets, farmers might work with local craftspeople or attend craft fairs.

CHAPTER EIGHT

Marketing Strategies

Effective marketing methods are essential for promoting alpaca fiber products. Emphasizing the natural and ecological qualities of alpaca husbandry, as well as the quality of the fiber, may appeal to environmentally aware customers. Online platforms, farmer's markets, and partnerships with local businesses are all viable methods to reach a larger audience.

Finally, alpaca farming includes the birthing process, rearing alpaca crias, fiber gathering and processing, alpaca shearing procedures, and the use of alpaca fiber in different goods and markets. A thorough grasp of each component is critical to the overall profitability and sustainability of an alpaca farming enterprise.

Market Your Alpaca Farm

Alpaca farming may be a profitable endeavor, but success is typically dependent on good marketing methods. Whether you're an experienced alpaca farmer or just getting started, marketing your alpaca goods and services is critical for long-term success and development.

Developing A distinctive Brand Identity

Creating a distinct brand identity is the cornerstone of effective marketing. Begin by creating an engaging tale about your farm's history, values, and dedication to ethical alpaca farming. Consider developing a distinctive logo and eye-catching packaging for alpaca items. A unique brand identity enables your farm to stand out in a competitive market.

Online Presence and Social Media

In the digital era, having a strong online presence is unavoidable. Create a user-friendly website that highlights your alpaca farm's goods and services. Use social media networks like Instagram, Facebook, and Pinterest to connect with prospective consumers. Share beautiful photos of your alpacas, behind-the-scenes looks at farm life, and customer comments. Social media not only helps you develop a community around your company, but it also allows for direct consumer connection.

Partnerships And Collaborations

Explore collaborations with local companies or craftsmen to broaden your reach. Collaborate with fiber artisans to produce one-of-a-kind alpaca goods, or partner with local businesses to run collaborative promotions. Collaborations like this not only showcase your alpaca farm to new audiences but also develop community bonds. Consider participating at farmers' markets, artisan fairs, and other local events to meet prospective clients in person.

Financial Management And Budgeting

Effective financial management is essential for a profitable alpaca farm. Careful budgeting and financial planning are required to assure profitability and long-term viability.

Initial Investment and Operating Costs

Begin by determining the initial investment necessary to establish and operate your alpaca farm. Consider the expenses of obtaining alpacas, constructing shelters, purchasing equipment, and finding appropriate pasture. Consider continuing running expenditures, such as feed, veterinarian care, and basic upkeep. With a firm awareness of these financial issues, you may establish fair prices for your alpaca goods and services.

CHAPTER NINE

Diversification and Revenue Stream

Investigate diversification to increase income sources. In addition to selling alpaca fiber, you may provide farm tours, educational courses, or agrotourism experiences. Diversifying your products not only increases revenue but also improves the general attractiveness of your alpaca farm.

Keep track of your income sources and analyze their performance regularly to uncover opportunities for improvement.

Savings and Contingency Planning

Create a financial safety net by allocating a percentage of your earnings for savings. Unexpected obstacles, such as alpaca health concerns or market swings, may influence your farm's financial stability.

Having a contingency plan in place guarantees that you can get through challenging times without jeopardizing the health of your alpacas or the survival of your company.

Troubleshooting: Common Alpaca Farming Challenges

Alpaca farming, like any other agricultural enterprise, has its own set of problems. Anticipating and resolving these difficulties ahead of time is critical for your alpacas' health and your farm's performance.

Health and Veterinary Care

Alpacas need frequent veterinarian care to keep them healthy and disease-free. Stay educated about common alpaca health concerns, such as parasites and respiratory diseases, and collaborate with a trained veterinarian to develop a preventative care plan. Regular health checks, immunizations, and correct diet are all essential components of alpaca care.

Fiber Quality And Processing

Any alpaca farm's first objective is to produce high-quality alpaca fiber. To improve the quality of your alpaca's fiber, monitor their diet, groom them properly, and keep their living area clean. To increase the value of your alpaca goods, consider alternative processing techniques such as spinning, weaving, or felting. Collaborate with expert textile artisans to produce one-of-a-kind, marketable things.

Market Volatility And Demand Variability

The alpaca market may be impacted by a variety of variables, including fashion trends, changes in customer tastes, and financial situations. Be adaptive and ready to modify your marketing methods and product offers to suit changing demands. Building a loyal client base and establishing partnerships with local companies will help you maintain a consistent market presence even amid changes.

Success Stories Of Alpaca Farming

While there are inherent hurdles in alpaca farming, countless success stories show the potential for a flourishing and sustainable enterprise.

Breeding Success

Successful alpaca breeding programs have produced high-quality bloodlines and champion alpacas. Strategic breeding, guided by a thorough grasp of genetics, has produced alpacas with exceptional fiber properties and conformation. Highlighting the success of your breeding program will help attract customers and improve your farm's image in the alpaca community.

Innovative Product Development

Some alpaca farms have achieved success by innovating their product offers. From beautiful alpaca yarn to hypoallergenic bedding, inventive businesses have developed new ways to use alpaca fiber. To remain competitive, consider experimenting with new product ideas, soliciting consumer input, and constantly improving your products.

Community Engagement And Education

Alpaca farms that actively connect with their communities and focus on education often achieve long-term success. Hosting seminars on alpaca care, fiber processing, and sustainable farming techniques may help your farm gain a favorable reputation.

Educated customers are more likely to recognize the value of alpaca goods and contribute to your company's success.

Conclusion

Marketing, financial management, problem-solving, and learning from success stories are all necessary components of a profitable alpaca farm.

You may position your alpaca farm for success by creating a strong brand identity, using online and offline marketing methods, and building community relationships. Financial restraint, income diversification, and proactive troubleshooting assure your farm's long-term survival.

As you negotiate the world of alpaca farming, remember that every problem is a chance for progress, and every success story adds to the collective narrative of a thriving alpaca business.